ODD NUMBERS AND EVEN NUMBERS

1 **2** 3 **4** 5 **6** 7 **8** 9 **10** 1

All the numbers in **heavy ty** s'.

COUNTING DOWN

IN 8s

80 72 64 56 48 40 32 24 16 8 0

IN 9s

90 81 72 63 54 45 36 27 18 9 0

IN 10s

100 90 80 70 60 50 40 30 20 10 0

IN 11s

110 99 88 77 66 55 44 33 22 11 0

IN 12s

120 108 96 84 72 60 48 36 24 12 0

IN 20s

200 180 160 140 120 100 80 60 40 20 0

MESSAGE TO PARENTS

These books are designed to help children in the 6-8 age range to learn and practice their early maths skills. Basic facts about addition, subtraction, multiplication and division are presented in a clear and understandable way with the use of amusing, colourful pictures, simple text and numerous games and puzzles. In this way the books can be used in the home to complement and reinforce the educational process that takes place in school.

Knowledge absorbed gradually is usually absorbed more thoroughly, so never try to cover too much in one session. It is important to make sure that your child understands each page as you progress together through the books. Always remember that learning ought to be an enjoyable experience and, in particular, that maths can be and should be FUN.

First published 1995 by Brown Watson
The Old Mill, Fleckney Road
Kibworth Beauchamp, Leics LE8 0HG
© 1995 Brown Watson
ISBN: 0-7097-1084-4

division

Compiled by Colin Clark
Illustrated by Stephen Holmes

Brown Watson
ENGLAND

Here are two balloons.

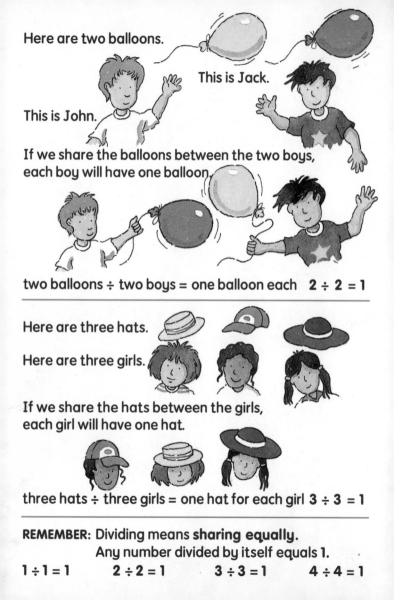

This is John.

This is Jack.

If we share the balloons between the two boys, each boy will have one balloon.

two balloons ÷ two boys = one balloon each **2 ÷ 2 = 1**

Here are three hats.

Here are three girls.

If we share the hats between the girls, each girl will have one hat.

three hats ÷ three girls = one hat for each girl **3 ÷ 3 = 1**

REMEMBER: Dividing means **sharing equally.**
Any number divided by itself equals **1.**

1 ÷ 1 = 1   **2 ÷ 2 = 1**   **3 ÷ 3 = 1**   **4 ÷ 4 = 1**

Here are four balloons.

Here are two boys.

If we share the balloons between the two boys,
each boy will have two balloons.

four balloons ÷ two boys = two balloons each **4 ÷ 2 = 2**

Here are eight gloves.

Here are two girls.

If we share the gloves between the girls,
each girl will have four gloves.

eight gloves ÷ two girls = four gloves each **8 ÷ 2 = 4**

REMEMBER: You can only divide even numbers by **2**.
You cannot divide odd numbers by **2**.

2 ÷ 2 = 1   6 ÷ 2 = 3   8 ÷ 2 = 4   5 ÷ 2 = no

Here are six coconuts.

Here are three monkeys.

If they share the coconuts equally,
each monkey will have two coconuts.

six coconuts ÷ three monkeys = two coconuts each

$$6 \div 3 = 2$$

If there are six coconuts,

and two monkeys,

each monkey will have three coconuts.

six coconuts ÷ two monkeys = three coconuts each

$$6 \div 2 = 3$$

REMEMBER: Any number divided by **1** remains the same.

$6 \div 1 = 6$ $5 \div 1 = 5$ $2 \div 1 = 2$ $1 \div 1 = 1$

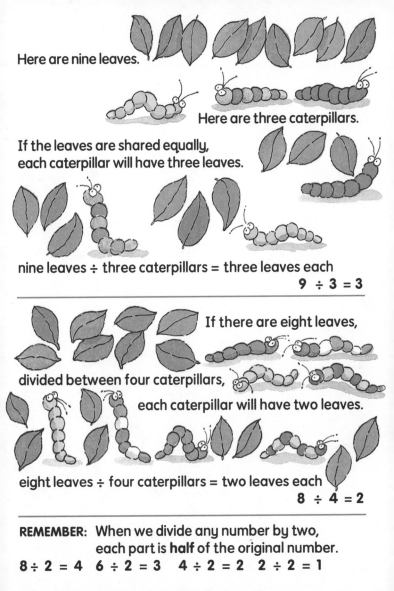

Here are nine leaves.

Here are three caterpillars.

If the leaves are shared equally,
each caterpillar will have three leaves.

nine leaves ÷ three caterpillars = three leaves each

9 ÷ 3 = 3

If there are eight leaves,

divided between four caterpillars,

each caterpillar will have two leaves.

eight leaves ÷ four caterpillars = two leaves each

8 ÷ 4 = 2

REMEMBER: When we divide any number by two,
each part is **half** of the original number.

8 ÷ 2 = 4   6 ÷ 2 = 3   4 ÷ 2 = 2   2 ÷ 2 = 1

There are ten bones on the ground,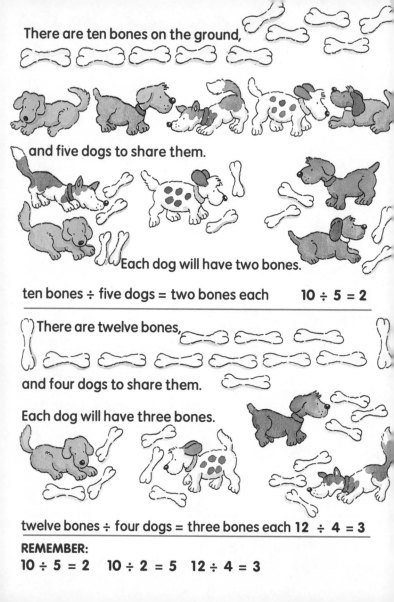

and five dogs to share them.

Each dog will have two bones.

ten bones ÷ five dogs = two bones each $10 ÷ 5 = 2$

There are twelve bones,

and four dogs to share them.

Each dog will have three bones.

twelve bones ÷ four dogs = three bones each $12 ÷ 4 = 3$

REMEMBER:
$10 ÷ 5 = 2$ $10 ÷ 2 = 5$ $12 ÷ 4 = 3$

If we divide fourteen pieces of cheese

between seven mice,

each mouse will have two pieces of cheese.

fourteen pieces of cheese ÷ seven mice =
two pieces of cheese for each mouse   **14 ÷ 7 = 2**

If we divide twenty-one pieces of cheese,

between seven mice,

each mouse will have three pieces of cheese.

twenty-one pieces of cheese ÷ seven mice =
three pieces of cheese for each mouse   **21 ÷ 7 = 3**

REMEMBER:
14 ÷ 7 = 2   14 ÷ 2 = 7   21 ÷ 7 = 3

Parachute puzzle

Which plane has each parachute come from?
Find out by answering the sums on the sides of the planes.

Sharing sums

The answers are at the foot of the page.

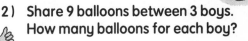

1) Share 10 coconuts between 5 monkeys.
How many coconuts for each monkey?

2) Share 9 balloons between 3 boys.
How many balloons for each boy?

3) Share 20 chocolates between 4 girls.
How many chocolates will each girl have?

4) Share 30 eggs between 6 nests.
How many eggs in each nest?

5) Share 24 fish between 4 fishbowls.
How many fish in each bowl?

6) Share 40 carrots between 5 rabbits.
How many carrots can each rabbit eat?

Answers:

1) $10 \div 5 = 2$ 2) $9 \div 3 = 3$ 3) $20 \div 4 = 5$

4) $30 \div 6 = 5$ 5) $24 \div 4 = 6$ 6) $40 \div 5 = 8$

Here are twenty-four bottles.

Each of these crates will hold six bottles.

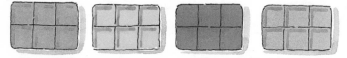

How many crates will we need for them?

twenty-four bottles ÷ six (bottles in a crate) =
four crates   **24 ÷ 6 = 4**

If we have thirty bottles, we will fill five crates.

thirty bottles ÷ six (bottles in a crate) = five crates
                                              30 ÷ 6 = 5

REMEMBER: Only numbers which end with a **5** or a **0** can
            be divided by **5**.

5   10   15   20   25   30   35   40   45   50   55   60

Here are thirty-six eggs.

Each of these hens has laid the same number of eggs.

How many eggs has each hen laid?
thirty-six eggs ÷ six hens =
six eggs for each hen

36 ÷ 6 = 6

Here are forty-two ducklings.

If there are seven ducks,

how many ducklings belong to each duck?

forty-two ducklings ÷ seven ducks =
six ducklings for each duck

42 ÷ 7 = 6

REMEMBER:

36 ÷ 6 = 6   **42 ÷ 7 = 6**

If there are forty-nine carrots,

and seven hungry rabbits,

how many carrots will each rabbit have?

forty-nine carrots ÷ seven rabbits =
seven carrots for each rabbit   **49 ÷ 7 = 7**

These fifty-six tadpoles

belong to these eight frogs.

How many tadpoles does each frog have?

fifty-six tadpoles ÷ eight frogs =
seven tadpoles for each frog   **56 ÷ 8 = 7**

REMEMBER:

49 ÷ 7 = 7   56 ÷ 8 = 7

There are sixty-four bees in this swarm.

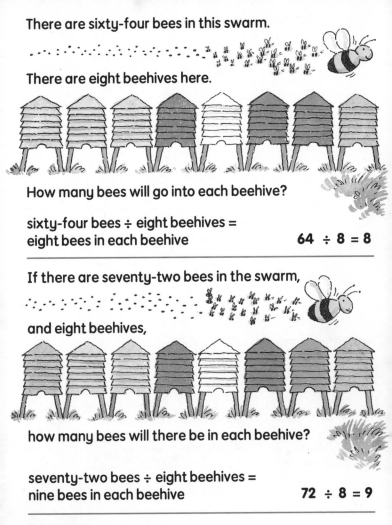

There are eight beehives here.

How many bees will go into each beehive?

sixty-four bees ÷ eight beehives =
eight bees in each beehive   **64 ÷ 8 = 8**

If there are seventy-two bees in the swarm,

and eight beehives,

how many bees will there be in each beehive?

seventy-two bees ÷ eight beehives =
nine bees in each beehive   **72 ÷ 8 = 9**

REMEMBER:

64 ÷ 8 = 8   72 ÷ 8 = 9

Can you do these sums?

The answers are at the foot of the page.

1) 7 ÷ 7

2) 9 ÷ 1

3) 12 ÷ 3

4) 14 ÷ 2

5) 20 ÷ 4

6) 24 ÷ 6

7) 28 ÷ 4

8) 30 ÷ 5

9) 36 ÷ 6

10) 42 ÷ 7

11) 45 ÷ 5

12) 49 ÷ 7

13) 56 ÷ 8

14) 64 ÷ 8

15) 72 ÷ 9

Answers:

1) 1   2) 9   3) 4   4) 7   5) 5   6) 4   7) 7   8) 6
9) 6   10) 6   11) 9   12) 7   13) 7   14) 8   15) 8

Can you fill in the missing numbers?

The answers are at the foot of the page.

1) 5 ÷ ☐ = 1

2) 3 ÷ ☐ = 3

3) 8 ÷ ☐ = 4

4) 6 ÷ ☐ = 2

5) ☐ ÷ 7 = 3

6) ☐ ÷ 6 = 4

7) ☐ ÷ 9 = 5

8) ☐ ÷ 8 = 6

9) ☐ ÷ 5 = 5

10) 36 ÷ ☐ = 4

11) 66 ÷ ☐ = 11

12) 54 ÷ ☐ = 6

13) ☐ ÷ 7 = 9

14) ☐ ÷ 4 = 12

15) 49 ÷ ☐ = 7

If we share seventy chocolates

between ten children,

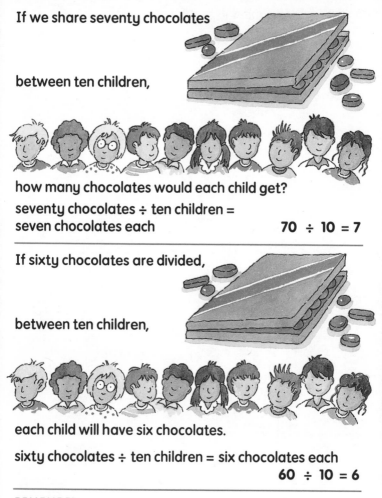

how many chocolates would each child get?

seventy chocolates ÷ ten children =
seven chocolates each   **70 ÷ 10 = 7**

If sixty chocolates are divided,

between ten children,

each child will have six chocolates.

sixty chocolates ÷ ten children = six chocolates each
                                    60 ÷ 10 = 6

REMEMBER:

Only numbers which end with a **0** can be divided by **10**.

10   20   30   40   50   60   70   80   90   100

If we divide twelve balls

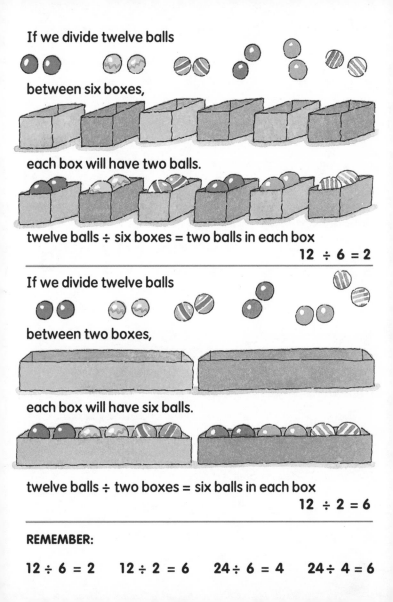

between six boxes,

each box will have two balls.

twelve balls ÷ six boxes = two balls in each box

12 ÷ 6 = 2

If we divide twelve balls

between two boxes,

each box will have six balls.

twelve balls ÷ two boxes = six balls in each box

12 ÷ 2 = 6

REMEMBER:

12 ÷ 6 = 2   12 ÷ 2 = 6   24 ÷ 6 = 4   24 ÷ 4 = 6

We can divide some numbers in lots of different ways.

Here are 24 beads divided by twenty-four. **24 ÷ 24 = 1**

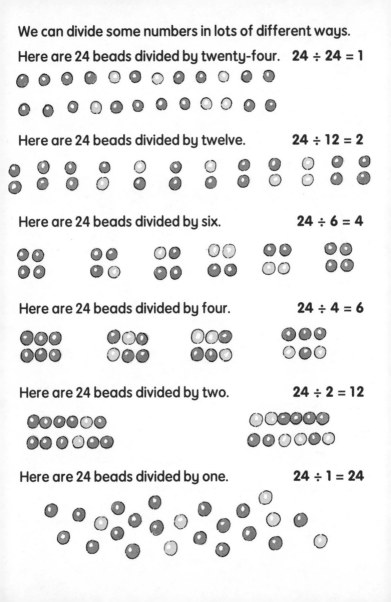

Here are 24 beads divided by twelve. **24 ÷ 12 = 2**

Here are 24 beads divided by six. **24 ÷ 6 = 4**

Here are 24 beads divided by four. **24 ÷ 4 = 6**

Here are 24 beads divided by two. **24 ÷ 2 = 12**

Here are 24 beads divided by one. **24 ÷ 1 = 24**

Here is another number that can be divided in different ways.

Here are 30 sweets divided by thirty.   **30 ÷ 30 = 1**

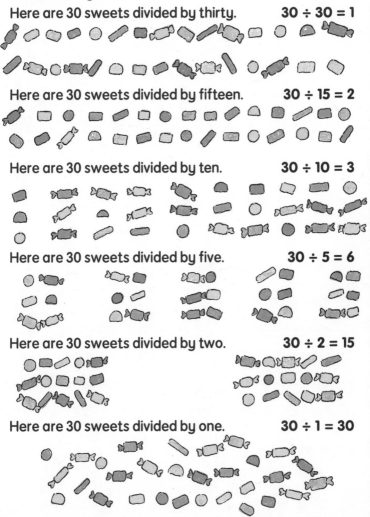

Here are 30 sweets divided by fifteen.   **30 ÷ 15 = 2**

Here are 30 sweets divided by ten.   **30 ÷ 10 = 3**

Here are 30 sweets divided by five.   **30 ÷ 5 = 6**

Here are 30 sweets divided by two.   **30 ÷ 2 = 15**

Here are 30 sweets divided by one.   **30 ÷ 1 = 30**

Dividing and sharing quiz

Can you answer these questions?
Look at the foot of the page to see if you are right.

A) 36 flowers

1) How many 12s? 2) How many 9s?

3) How many 6s? 4) How many 4s?

5) How many 3s? 6) How many 2s?

B) 40 arrows

1) How many 20s? 2) How many 10s?

3) How many 8s? 4) How many 5s?

5) How many 4s? 6) How many 2s?

C) 48 rockets

1) How many 24s? 2) How many 16s?

3) How many 12s? 4) How many 8s?

5) How many 6s? 6) How many 4s?

7) How many 3s? 8) How many 2s?

Answers:

A)	1) 3	2) 4	3) 6	4) 9	5) 12	6) 18
B)	1) 2	2) 4	3) 5	4) 8	5) 10	6) 20
C)	1) 2	2) 3	3) 4	4) 6	5) 8	6) 12	7) 16	8) 24

Camel calculations

This camel has six loads to carry. Each load is made up of 4 boxes. Work out the sums on the side of each box and add them together to see what each load weighs. The camel cannot carry a load that weighs more than 20. Which load is too heavy for it?

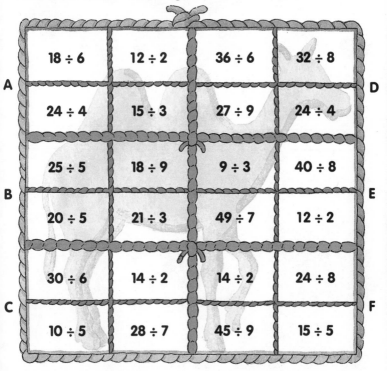

A	$18 \div 6$	$12 \div 2$	$36 \div 6$	$32 \div 8$	**D**
	$24 \div 4$	$15 \div 3$	$27 \div 9$	$24 \div 4$	
B	$25 \div 5$	$18 \div 9$	$9 \div 3$	$40 \div 8$	**E**
	$20 \div 5$	$21 \div 3$	$49 \div 7$	$12 \div 2$	
C	$30 \div 6$	$14 \div 2$	$14 \div 2$	$24 \div 8$	**F**
	$10 \div 5$	$28 \div 7$	$45 \div 9$	$15 \div 5$	

Answers:

Load E is too heavy for the camel to carry.

A) $3 + 6 + 6 + 5 = 20$ B) $5 + 2 + 4 + 7 = 18$
C) $5 + 7 + 2 + 4 = 18$ D) $6 + 4 + 3 + 6 = 19$
E) $3 + 5 + 7 + 6 = 21$ F) $7 + 3 + 5 + 3 = 18$

If there are 33 cherries
to be shared out between 11 children,

there will be 3 cherries for each child.

thirty-three cherries ÷ eleven children =
three cherries each

$33 \div 11 = 3$

If there are 33 cherries
to be shared out between 3 children,

each child will get 11 cherries.

thirty-three cherries ÷ three children =
eleven cherries each

$33 \div 3 = 11$

REMEMBER:

$33 \div 11 = 3$ $33 \div 3 = 11$ $99 \div 11 = 9$ $99 \div 9 = 11$

Here are 60 seeds.

Here are 12 ants.

If they share the seeds, each ant will get 5.

sixty seeds ÷ twelve ants = five seeds for each ant

60 ÷ 12 = 5

If there are 120 seeds,

and 12 ants,

each ant will have 10 seeds.

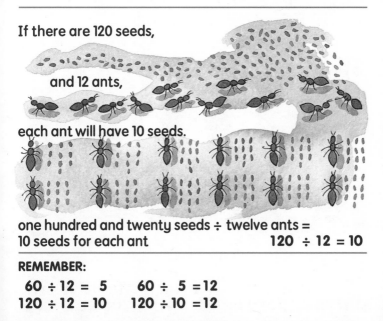

one hundred and twenty seeds ÷ twelve ants =
10 seeds for each ant   **120 ÷ 12 = 10**

REMEMBER:

60 ÷ 12 = 5	**60 ÷ 5 = 12**
120 ÷ 12 = 10	**120 ÷ 10 = 12**

Can you fill in the missing numbers?

The answers are at the foot of the page.

1) $60 \div \quad = 6$

2) $\quad \div 9 = 10$

3) $84 \div 12 =$

4) $48 \div \quad = 12$

5) $64 \div 8 =$

6) $\quad \div 6 = 20$

7) $81 \div \quad = 9$

8) $\quad \div 7 = 11$

9) $108 \div \quad = 12$

10) $132 \div 11 =$

11) $\quad \div 9 = 7$

12) $121 \div \quad = 11$

13) $56 \div 7 =$

14) $\quad \div 12 = 6$

15) $144 \div \quad = 12$

What can they buy?

The answers are at the foot of the page.

Jack has 50 pence.

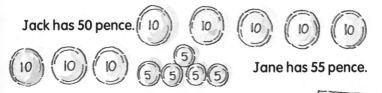

Jane has 55 pence.

1) How many buns can Jack buy?
   How much money will he be left with?

   BUNS
   9p

   CREAM CAKES
   15p

2) How many cream cakes can Jane buy?
   Will she have enough money left to buy a doughnut?

3) If Jack decides to buy doughnuts instead of buns,
   how many can he afford?

   DOUGHNUTS
   10p

4) How many tarts can Jane buy?

   TARTS
   11p

5) If Jane buys two buns and two tarts, will she
   have enough money for a cream cake as well?

Answers:

1) 5 buns; 5 pence left   2) 3 cream cakes; yes, she has
10 pence left for a doughnut   3) 5 doughnuts   4) 5 tarts
5) 2 buns cost 18 pence, 2 tarts cost 22 pence, total
40 pence. Jane has 15 pence left, enough for a cream cake.

ODD NUMBERS AND EVEN NUMBERS

1 2 **3** 4 **5** 6 **7** 8 **9** 10 **11** 12 **13** 14 **15** 16 **17** 18 **19** 20

All the numbers in **heavy type** are called the 'odd numbers'.

COUNTING DOWN

IN 2s

30 28 26 24 22 20 18 16 14 12 10 8 6 4 2 0

IN 3s

30 27 24 21 18 15 12 9 6 3 0

IN 4s

40 36 32 28 24 20 16 12 8 4 0

IN 5s

50 45 40 35 30 25 20 15 10 5 0

IN 6s

60 54 48 42 36 30 24 18 12 6 0

IN 7s

70 63 56 49 42 35 28 21 14 7 0